Contents

The World

ATLAS LEGEND

⊛ National capital
★ State or province capital
• Other city
▲ Mountain peak
━ National border
─ State or province border
---- Boundry in dispute

ARCTIC OCEAN

180° 160° 140° 120° 100° 80° 60° 40°

80°

60°

Greenland
(Denmark)

ALASKA
(U.S.)

ICEL

IRELA

CANADA

NORTH
AMERICA

40°

UNITED STATES

Azores
(Portugal)

PORTU

ATLANTIC

OCEAN

MOROC

Bermuda
(U.K.)

Canary Is.
(Spain)

20°

Tropic of Cancer

MEXICO

BAHAMAS

WESTERN
SAHARA
(Morocco)

Midland
Islands
(U.S.)

HAWAII
(U.S.)

PACIFIC

OCEAN

CUBA
HAITI DOMINICAN
REP.
PUERTO RICO (U.S.)

CAPE VERDE

MAURITANI

BELIZE
HONDURAS
JAMAICA

SENEGAL

GUATEMALA

THE
GAMBIA GUINEA

EL SALVADOR NICARAGUA

BARBADOS

GUINEA–
BISSAU SIERRA
LEONE

COSTA
RICA

TRINIDAD AND TOBAGO
GUYANA

LIBERI

PANAMA

VENEZUELA

SURINAME

CÔTE
D'IVOIR

COLOMBIA

FRENCH GUIANA
(France)

Equator

ECUADOR

Galápagos
Islands
(Ecuador)

BRAZIL

SOUTH

Tokelau
(N.Z.)

KIRIBATI

PERU

AMERICA

American
Samoa
(U.S.)

SAMOA

French
Polynesia
(France)

BOLIVIA

Cook
Islands
(N.Z.)

PARAGUAY

20°

TONGA

Pitcairn
(U.K.)

Tropic of Capricorn

CHILE

ATLANTIC

Niue
(N.Z.)

Easter Island
(Chile)

OCEAN

URUGUAY

ARGENTINA

40°

PACIFIC

Falkland
Islands
(U.K.)

South
Georgia
(U.K.)

OCEAN

60°

Antarctic Circle

80°

180° 160° 140° 120° 100° 80° 60° 40°

* The former Yugoslav Republic of Macedonia

ARCTIC OCEAN

Arctic Circle

RUSSIA

ASIA

NORWAY SWEDEN FINLAND

ESTONIA
LATVIA
LITH.
DEN. POLAND BELARUS
NETH.
BEL. CZECH
GER. REP.
EUROPE SLOVAKIA UKRAINE
SWITZ. AUS. HUN. ROM. MOLD.
FRANCE SLOV.
CROATIA SERB. &
BOS. & HER. MONT. BUL.
ITALY ALB. F.Y.R.
MAC.
GREECE TURKEY

KAZAKHSTAN

MONGOLIA

NORTH
KOREA
JAPAN
SOUTH
KOREA

UZBEKISTAN
KYRGYZSTAN
GEORGIA
ARMENIA
AZERBAIJAN TAJIKISTAN
TURKMENISTAN

CHINA

PACIFIC
OCEAN

CYPRUS SYRIA
LEBANON AFGHANISTAN
ISRAEL IRAQ
JORDAN IRAN
KUWAIT NEPAL BHUTAN
PAKISTAN

TUNISIA

40°

20°

BAHRAIN QATAR
ALGERIA LIBYA EGYPT SAUDI U.A.E.
ARABIA OMAN INDIA BANGL.
MYANMAR LAOS
(BURMA) TAIWAN

Northern
Mariana Islands
(U.S.)

MALI NIGER CHAD SUDAN
ERITREA YEMEN
BURKINA THAI. VIETNAM PHILIPPINES
AFRICA DJIBOUTI CAMB.
SO BENIN
NIGERIA CENTRAL
EQU. AFRICAN REPUBLIC ETHIOPIA
GUINEA SRI
LANKA BRUNEI
CAMEROON SOMALIA MALDIVES
TOGO UGANDA MALAYSIA
ANA GABON REP. RWANDA KENYA
O TOME CONGO
NCIPE DEM. REP. BURUNDI
CONGO
CABINDA TANZANIA SEYCHELLES SINGAPORE
(Angola)
ANGOLA MALAWI COMOROS
ZAMBIA
MOZAMBIQUE MADAGASCAR
ZIMBABWE
NAMIBIA MAURITIUS
BOTSWANA
Réunion
(France)
SOUTH SWAZILAND
AFRICA LESOTHO

Guam (U.S.)

MARSHALL
ISLANDS

PALAU FEDERATED
STATES OF
MICRONESIA

INDONESIA

NAURU
KIRIBATI

PAPUA
NEW GUINEA

TUVALU

EAST
TIMOR

SOLOMON
ISLANDS

VANUATU FIJI

New
Caledonia
(France)

INDIAN
OCEAN

0°

20°

AUSTRALIA

1:81,500,000

0   1,000   2,000 Miles
0 500 1,000 1,500 Kilometers
Projection: Winkel
© MapQuest.com, Inc.

*Kerguelen
Islands
(France)*

NEW
ZEALAND

60°

ANTARCTICA

80°

United States

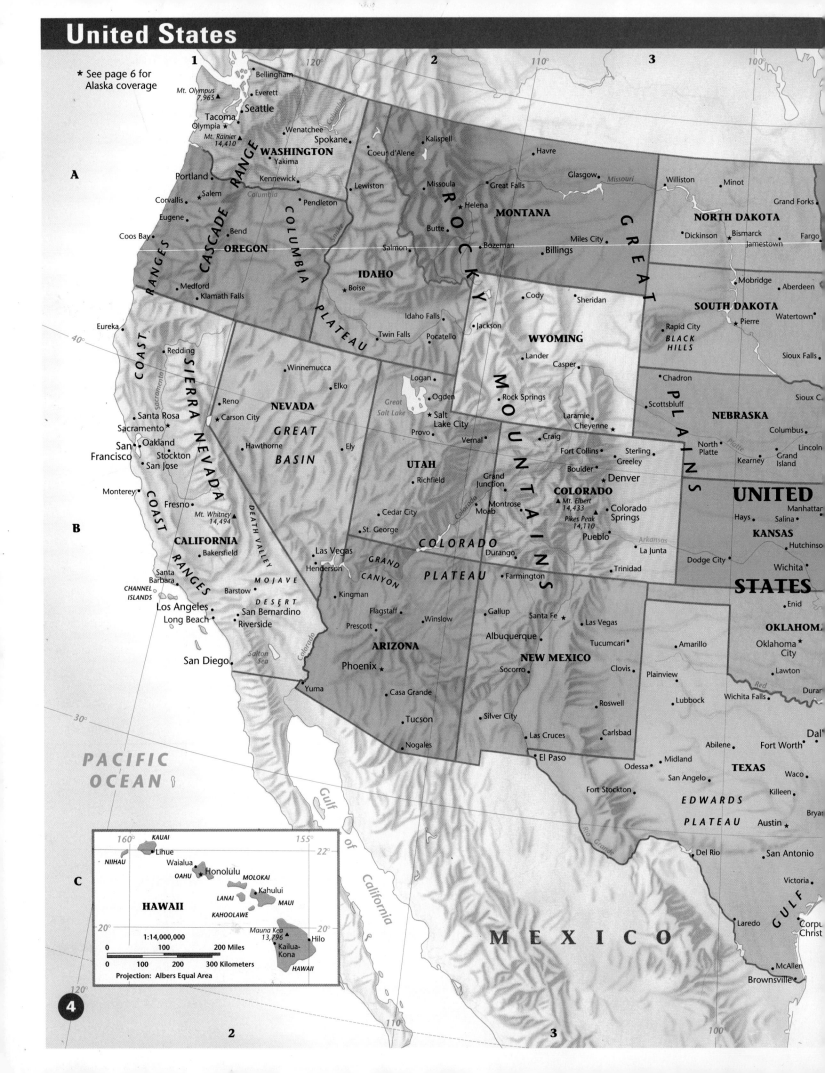

*See page 6 for Alaska coverage

1   120°   **2**   110°   **3**   100°

Bellingham
Mt. Olympus 7,965 ▲
Everett
Tacoma •Seattle
Olympia ★
Mt. Rainier 14,410 ▲
Wenatchee
Spokane
Kalispell
Havre
Glasgow   *Missouri*
Williston
Minot

A

Portland •
Yakima
WASHINGTON
Coeur d'Alene
Missoula
Great Falls
Grand Forks

Corvallis •
Salem
Columbia
Lewiston
Helena
MONTANA
Dickinson Bismarck
Fargo
NORTH DAKOTA
Jamestown

Eugene •
Pendleton
Butte
Billings
Miles City

Coos Bay •
Bend
OREGON
Salmon
Bozeman
Mobridge
Aberdeen

Medford •
Boise ★
Cody
Sheridan
SOUTH DAKOTA

Klamath Falls •
Idaho Falls
Jackson •
WYOMING
Rapid City
BLACK HILLS
★ Pierre
Watertown

40°
Eureka •
Twin Falls
Pocatello
Lander •
Casper
Sioux Falls

Redding •
NEVADA
Winnemucca
Logan •
Ogden •
Rock Springs •
Chadron •
Scottsbluff •
Sioux C.

Reno •
Elko •
Great Salt Lake
★ Salt Lake City
Laramie •
Cheyenne ★
North Platte
NEBRASKA
Columbus •
Lincoln •

★ Carson City
GREAT BASIN
Hawthorne •
Ely •
Provo •
Vernal •
Craig •
Fort Collins •
Sterling •
Greeley
Kearney •
Grand Island

Santa Rosa •
Sacramento ★
San Francisco
Oakland
Stockton
San Jose
UTAH
Richfield •
Grand Junction
Boulder •
Denver
COLORADO
Mt. Elbert 14,433 ▲
Hays •
Salina •
Manhattan

Monterey •
Fresno •
Mt. Whitney 14,494
Cedar City •
Montrose •
Moab
Pikes Peak 14,110
Colorado Springs
KANSAS
Hutchins

B
CALIFORNIA
Bakersfield •
DEATH VALLEY
St. George •
COLORADO PLATEAU
Durango •
Pueblo
Arkansas
La Junta •
Trinidad •
Dodge City •
Wichita •

Santa Barbara •
Las Vegas
Henderson
GRAND CANYON
Farmington •

CHANNEL ISLANDS
Barstow •
MOJAVE DESERT
Kingman •
Gallup •
Santa Fe ★
Las Vegas •
Amarillo •
Enid •

Los Angeles
Long Beach
San Bernardino
Riverside
Flagstaff •
Winslow •
Albuquerque
Tucumcari •
OKLAHOMA
Oklahoma ★ City

San Diego •
Salton Sea
Prescott •
ARIZONA
NEW MEXICO
Clovis •
Plainview •
Lawton •

Yuma •
Phoenix ★
Casa Grande •
Socorro •
Roswell •
Lubbock •
Wichita Falls •
Durar

30°
Tucson •
Silver City •
Carlsbad •
Abilene •
Fort Worth •
Dal

Nogales •
Las Cruces •
Odessa •
Midland •
TEXAS
Waco •

El Paso •
San Angelo •
Fort Stockton •
Killeen •
Bryar

PACIFIC OCEAN

UNITED STATES

Gulf of California

EDWARDS PLATEAU
Austin ★

Rio Grande
Del Rio •
San Antonio •

M E X I C O

Laredo •
Victoria •

Corpus Christ

McAllen •
Brownsville •

4

HAWAII inset

160°   *KAUAI*   155°
NIIHAU   Lihue •
Waialua
OAHU ★ Honolulu
22°

MOLOKAI
Kahului •
LANAI   *MAUI*
HAWAII
KAHOOLAWE

20°
Mauna Kea 13,796 ▲
Hilo •
Kailua-Kona •
HAWAII

1:14,000,000
0   100   200 Miles
0   100   200   300 Kilometers
Projection: Albers Equal Area

2   110°   **3**   100°

Canada and Alaska

RUSSIA

Chukchi Sea

Bering Sea

Bering Strait

ARCTIC OCEAN

ST. LAWRENCE ISLAND

POINT HOPE
• Point Hope

• Barrow   POINT BARROW

PRINCE PATRICK ISLAND

QUEEN

Norton Sound
• Nome
• Kotzebue

• Prudhoe Bay

Beaufort Sea

MELVILLE ISLAND

BROOKS RANGE

BANKS ISLAND

Viscount Melville Sound

NUNIVAK ISLAND

ALASKA (United States)

• Sachs Harbour

VICTORIA ISLAND

Amundsen Gulf

• Bethel   • Holy Cross

• Tuktoyaktuk

• Fort Yukon

• Inuvik

Yukon

• College
• Fairbanks

Mt. McKinley
20,320 ▲

• Fort McPherson

• Cambridge Bay

• Dillingham

ALASKA RANGE

Great Bear Lake

• Kugluktuk

Bristol Bay

• Kenai   • Wasilla
• Anchorage

• Tok

• Dawson

• Déline

Mackenzie

• Homer
• Seward • Valdez
• Cordova

YUKON TERRITORY

Corppermine

Back

ALASKA PENINSULA

KODIAK ISLAND

• Kodiak

Gulf of Alaska

Mt. Logan
▲ 19,551

• Carmacks

Yukon

Pelly

NORTHWEST TERRITORIES

Thelon

• Whitehorse ★

Lac la Martre

PACIFIC OCEAN

• Haines • Skagway

• Watson Lake

• Fort Simpson

• Edzo • Yellowknife ★

Great Slave Lake

Dubawnt

Juneau ★

COAST MOUNTAINS

• Fort Liard

• Sitka

Stikine

• Hay River

• Fort Smith

• Petersburg
• Wrangell

• Fort Nelson

ROCKY MOUNTAINS

Hoy

• Ketchikan

• Stewart

Skeena

Williston Lake

• Fort Vermilion

Lake Claire

Lake Athabasca

Wollaston Lake

• Prince Rupert

• Kitimat

QUEEN CHARLOTTE ISLANDS

BRITISH COLUMBIA

Nechako Reservoir

• Prince George

• Fort St. John

Peace

• Dawson Creek

• Peace River

• Grand Prairie

• Fort McMurray

• La Loche

Reindeer Lake

SASKATCHEWAN

Churchill

Queen Charlotte Sound

ALBERTA

Athabasca

• La Ronge

Lac la Ronge

• Flin Flon

The Pa

Fraser

• Williams Lake

• Jasper

• Edmonton ★

N. Saskatchewan

• Prince Albert

• Saskatoon

VANCOUVER ISLAND

• Kamloops

• Red Deer

GREAT PLAINS

La

Winnipegos

• Nanaimo

• Vancouver • Kelowna

• Banff

• Calgary

Assiniboine

• Victoria ★

1:15,800,000

0   250   500 Miles
0   250   500   750 Kilometers

Projection: Azimuthal Equal Area
© MapQuest.com, Inc.

• Lethbridge

• Medicine Hat

S. Saskatchewan

Qu'Appelle

• Moose Jaw

★ Regina

UNITED

6

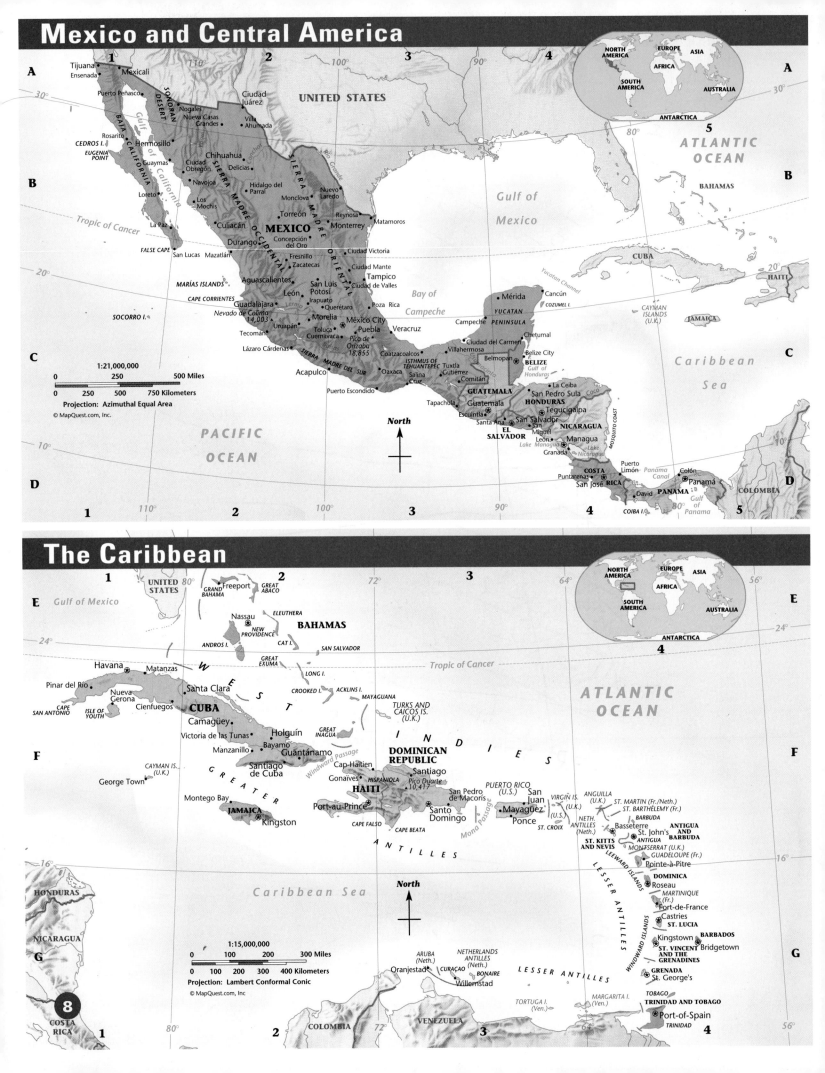

Mexico and Central America

The Caribbean

South America

A 1 B 2 3 4 5 6

HONDURAS
NICARAGUA
COSTA RICA
PANAMA

NORTH AMERICA EUROPE ASIA
AFRICA
SOUTH AMERICA
ANTARCTICA
AUSTRALIA

A

ARUBA (Neth.)
BONAIRE (Neth.)
CURAÇAO (Neth.)
GRENADA
BARBADOS
TRINIDAD & TOBAGO

Santa Marta
Barranquilla
Maracaibo
Coro
Valencia Caracas
Cumana
Cartagena
Valledupar
Lake Maracaibo
Cabimas
Maracay
Maturín
Sincelejo
Mérida
Barquisimeto
El Tigre
Montería
Valera
Ciudad Guayana
Cúcuta
San Cristóbal
San Fernando de Apure
Ciudad Bolívar
Georgetown
New Amsterdam
Paramaribo
Barrancabermeja
Bucaramanga
Kourou
Cayenne
Medellín
Puerto Ayacucho
VENEZUELA
GUYANA
SURINAME
FRENCH GUIANA (Fr.)
Manizales
Tunja
GUIANA HIGHLANDS
Pereira
Bogotá
Armenia
Ibagué
Villavicencio
Boa Vista
Buenaventura
Cali
Palmira
COLOMBIA
Popayán
Neiva
Pasto
Florencia
Macapá

ATLANTIC OCEAN

B

Esmeraldas
Quito
Equator
Cotopaxi 19,347
MARAJÓ ISLAND
Portoviejo
Ambato
ECUADOR
Cuenca
Guayaquil
Machala
Iquitos
Benjamin Constant
Manaus
Santarém
Belém
São Luís
Parnaíba
Tumbes
Loja
Fortaleza
Talara
Yurimaguas
A M A Z O N
Sullana
Piura
AGUJA POINT
PERU
S E L V A S
Imperatriz
Teresina
Chiclayo
Cajamarca
Cruzeiro do Sul
B A S I N
Floriano
Juàzeiro do Norte
Natal
Trujillo
Pucallpa
Rio Branco
Pôrto Velho
BRAZIL
Campina Grande
João Pessoa
Chimbote
Huánuco
Guajará-Mirim
Recife
Petrolina
Cerro de Pasco
Cobija
Riberalta
Callao
Huancayo
Puerto Maldonado
MATO GROSSO
Gurupi
BRAZILIAN
Lima
Ayacucho
Cuzco
Trinidad
Cuiabá
Vitória da Conquista
Salvador
Ica
BOLIVIA
PLATEAU
Anápolis
Brasília
Itabuna
Ilhéus
Juliaca
Lake Titicaca
La Paz
Goiânia
Montes Claros
Teófilo Otoni
Puno
Cochabamba
Oruro
Jataí
Uberlândia
HIGHLANDS
Arequipa
Sucre
Corumbá
Belo Horizonte
Governador Valadares
Tacna
Lake Poopó
Potosí
Campo Grande
São José do Rio Prêto
Pico da Bandeira 9,482
Vitória
Arica
Grande
Iquique
Tarija
São Paulo
Ribeirão Prêto
Campinas
Juiz de Fora
Volta Redonda
Antofagasta
Calama
Concepción
Dourados
Londrina
Sorocaba
Niterói
Rio de Janeiro
Tropic of Capricorn
Santos

C

D

E

SAN AMBROSIO ISLAND (Chile)
SAN FÉLIX ISLAND (Chile)
Copiapó
San Salvador de Jujuy
Salta
Asunción
Formosa
Coronel Oviedo
PARAGUAY
Encarnación
Passo Fundo
CHILE
Catamarca
San Miguel de Tucumán
Resistencia
Corrientes
Posadas
Santo Tomé
Santa Maria
Caxias do Sul
Florianópolis
Joinville
La Serena
Santiago del Estero
La Rioja
Reconquista
Uruguaiana
Pôrto Alegre

ATLANTIC OCEAN

F

JUAN FERNÁNDEZ ISLANDS (Chile)
Cerro Aconcagua 22,834
Viña del Mar
Valparaíso
San Bernardo
Santiago
Rancagua
Córdoba
San Juan
Mendoza
Río Cuarto
San Rafael
Santa Fe
Paraná
Rosario
Junín
Buenos Aires
Avellaneda
La Plata
Concordia
Salto
Paysandú
Rivera
Pelotas
Melo
URUGUAY
Minas
Montevideo
Talca
Chillán
Santa Rosa
Azul
Mar del Plata
Talcahuano
Concepción
Bahía Blanca
Necochea
Temuco
ARGENTINA
Neuquén
Punta Alta
Valdivia
Viedma

G

Osorno
Puerto Montt
San Carlos de Bariloche
Trelew
Rawson
San Matías Gulf
VALDÉS PENINSULA
CHILOÉ ISLAND
North
CHONOS ARCHIPELAGO
Comodoro Rivadavia
Gulf of San Jorge
TAITAO PENINSULA
CAPE TRES PUNTAS

1:32,300,000
0 250 500 750 Miles
0 250 500 750 1,000 Kilometers
Projection: Bipolar Oblique Conic Conformal
© MapQuest.com, Inc.

H

Bahía Grande
Stanley
FALKLAND ISLANDS (U.K.) (ISLAS MALVINAS)
Río Gallegos
Strait of Magellan
Punta Arenas
TIERRA DEL FUEGO
Ushuaia
CAPE HORN
SOUTH GEORGIA (U.K.)

10

PACIFIC OCEAN

A N D E S

L L A N O S
Orinoco
Negro
Amazon
Putumayo
Marañón
Juruá
Purus
Madeira
Guaporé
Beni
Mamoré
Pilcomayo
Paraguay
Paraná
Tapajós
Xingu
Tocantins
Araguaia
São Francisco
Grande
Uruguay
Río de la Plata
LA MONTAÑA
ALTIPLANO
ATACAMA DESERT
GRAN CHACO
CAMPOS
PAMPAS
PATAGONIA

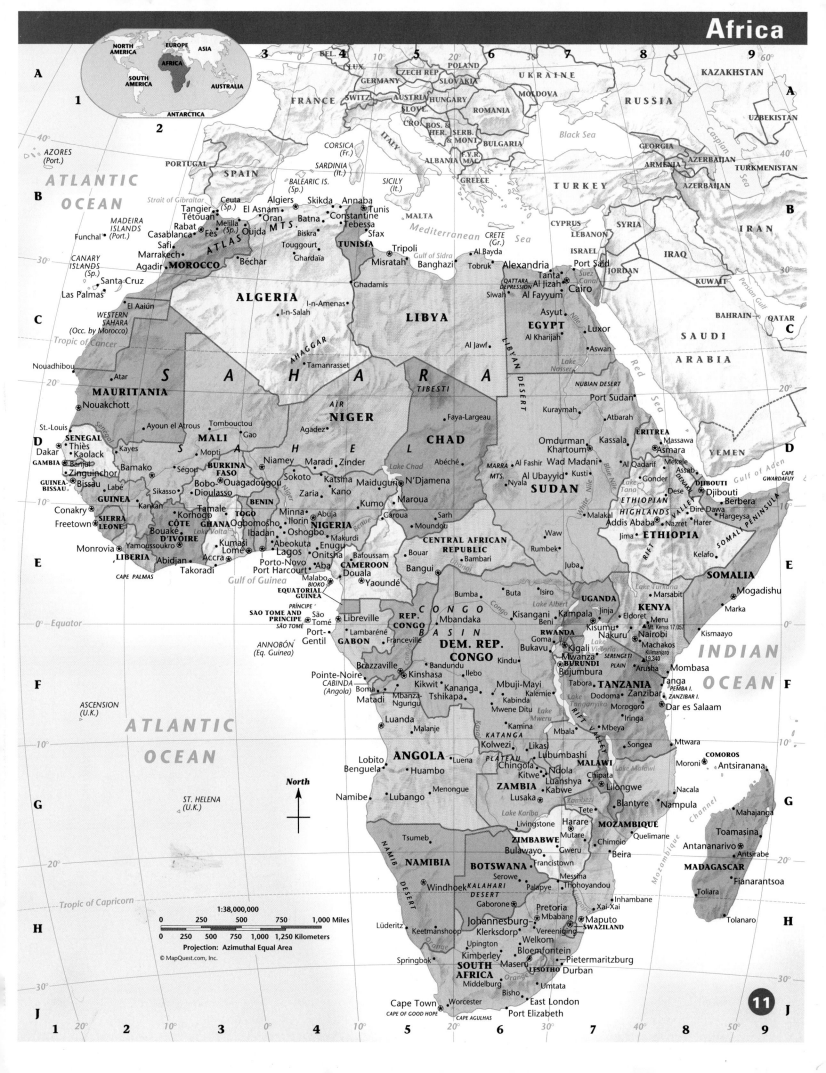

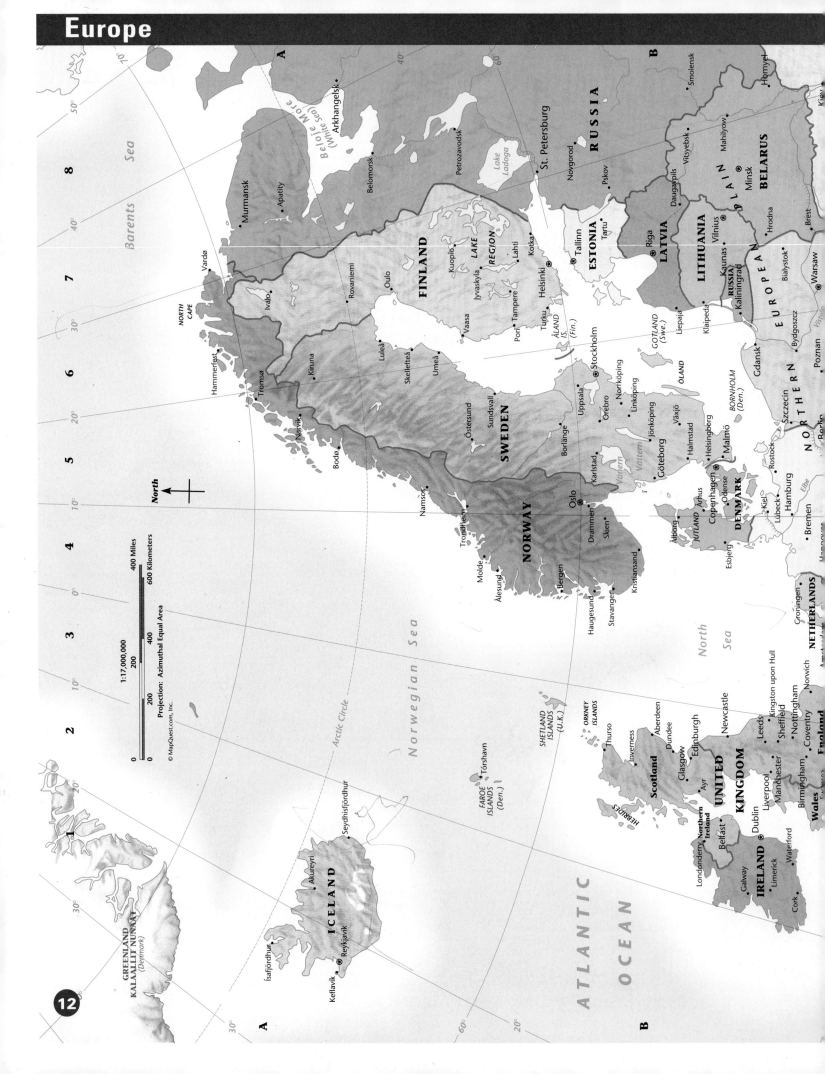

Barents Sea

Beloje More (White Sea)

Arkhangelsk

RUSSIA

Smolensk

Homyel

Murmansk
Apatity
Belomorsk

Vitsyebsk
Mahilyow
Minsk ⊛

BELARUS

St. Petersburg
Novgorod
Pskov

Petrozavodsk
Lake Ladoga

Daugavpils

Hrodna
Brest

FINLAND

Kuopio
LAKE REGION
Lahti
Kotka

Tallinn ⊛
ESTONIA
Tartu

Riga ⊛
LATVIA

LITHUANIA
Vilnius ⊛
Kaunas
Klaipeda
RUSSIA
Kaliningrad

Bialystok
Warsaw

Vardø

NORTH CAPE

Ivalo
Rovaniemi
Oulu

Jyväskylä
Vaasa
Tampere
Pori
Turku
Helsinki ⊛

ÅLAND IS. (Fin.)

GOTLAND (Swe.)
Liepaja

EUROPEAN

PLAIN

Bydgoszcz
Poznan

Hammerfest

Tromsø

Kiruna
Luleå
Skellefteå
Umeå

Stockholm ⊛
Uppsala
Örebro
Norrköping
Linköping

ÖLAND
BORNHOLM (Den.)
Gdansk

NORTHERN

Szczecin

Narvik
Bodø

Östersund
Sundsvall

SWEDEN

Borlänge
Karlstad
Jönköping
Göteborg
Halmstad
Helsingborg
Malmö

Rostock

Berlin

Namsos

North Sea

Trondheim

NORWAY

Oslo
Drammen
Skien

Vänern
Vättern
Väjsö

Copenhagen ⊛
DENMARK
Odense
Århus
Ålborg
JUTLAND
Kiel
Lübeck
Hamburg
Bremen

Elbe

North

← North

Molde
Ålesund
Bergen

Kristiansand
Haugesund
Stavanger

Esbjerg

Hannover

400 Miles
600 Kilometers

1:17,000,000
0   200   400
0   200   400

Projection: Azimuthal Equal Area

© MapQuest.com, Inc.

Norwegian Sea

NETHERLANDS
Groningen

Arctic Circle

SHETLAND ISLANDS (U.K.)

ORKNEY ISLANDS
Thurso
Inverness
Aberdeen
Dundee
Scotland
Glasgow
Edinburgh

Newcastle
Kingston upon Hull
Leeds
Sheffield
Nottingham
Norwich

FAROE ISLANDS (Den.)
Tórshavn

Ayr

UNITED
KINGDOM

Liverpool
Manchester

Birmingham
Coventry

Wales   England

HEBRIDES

GREENLAND
KALAALLIT NUNAAT
(Denmark)

Ísafjörðhur

Seyðisfjörðhur

ICELAND

Akureyri

Reykjavík ⊛
Keflavík

Londonderry
Northern Ireland
Belfast ⊛
Dublin ⊛

Galway
IRELAND
Limerick
Waterford
Cork

ATLANTIC

OCEAN

12

NORTH AMERICA
SOUTH AMERICA
EUROPE
AFRICA
ASIA
AUSTRALIA
ANTARCTICA

UKRAINE
Zhytomyr
Vinnytsya
Lviv
POLAND
Kielce
Wroclaw
Walbrzych
Katowice
Krakow
Liberec
Dresden
Leipzig
Erfurt
Chemnitz
GERMANY
Essen
Kassel
Cologne
Bonn
Frankfurt
Wiesbaden
Mannheim
Nürnberg
Plzen
Prague
CZECH REP.
Brno
Ostrava
Liberec
Regensburg
Saarbrücken
Stuttgart
Augsburg
Munich
Salzburg
Linz
Vienna
AUSTRIA
Graz
Klagenfurt
Innsbruck
Zürich
SWITZERLAND
Bern
Basel
Matterhorn
14,691
LIECHTENSTEIN

Moldova
Chisinau
Prut
Chernivtsi
Iasi
Galati
Constanta
Ploiesti
Bucharest
Brasov
Cluj-Napoca
Oradea
Debrecen
ROMANIA
CARPATHIAN MOUNTAINS
Timisoara
Szeged
Miskolc
Kosice
Banska Bystrica
SLOVAKIA
Bratislava
Gyor
Budapest
Kecskemet
HUNGARY
Pecs
Szombathely
Zagreb
CROATIA
Ljubljana
SLOVENIA
Rijeka
Udine
Trieste
Venice
DINARIC ALPS

Black Sea
30°
Varna
Ruse
Constanta
Pleven
BULGARIA
Sofia
Plovdiv
Stara Zagora
Kavala
Burgas
TURKEY
TURKEY
Novi Sad
Belgrade
SERBIA &
MONTENEGRO
Nis
Sarajevo
BOSNIA &
HERZEGOVINA
Banja Luka
Split
Dubrovnik
Podgorica
Shkoder
BALKAN
Skopje
F.Y.R. MAC.
Tirane
ALBANIA
Durrës
Vlore
CORFU
Thessaloniki
PENINSULA
Olympus
9,570
Ioannina
GREECE
Larisa
Volos
Sparta
Athens
Corinth
Patrai
PELOPONNESUS
Kalamai
CYCLADES
Sea of Crete
Iráklion
Khaniá
CRETE (Gr.)

30°
20°

Adriatic Sea
San Marino
SAN MARINO
Ancona
Bologna
Florence
Pisa
APENNINES
Rome
VATICAN CITY
Naples
Salerno
4,203
Vesuvius
ITALY
Foggia
Bari
Taranto
Ionian Sea
Reggio di Calabria
Messina
Etna
10,902
Catania
SICILY (It.)
Palermo
Tyrrhenian Sea
Cagliari
Sassari
SARDINIA (It.)
ELBA
CORSICA (Fr.)
Ajaccio
MONACO
Nice
Genoa
Turin
Milan
Bergamo
Verona
Parma
Po
Mt. Blanc
15,771
ALPS
Geneva
Lyon
Grenoble
Avignon
Toulon
Marseille

MALTA
Valletta

Mediterranean Sea
Gulf of Sidra
LIBYA

* F.Y.R. MAC. - The Former Yugoslav Republic of Macedonia

SWITZERLAND
Rhine
Strasbourg
Nancy
Dijon
FRANCE
Clermont-Ferrand
Saint-Étienne
Limoges
Montpellier
Toulouse
PYRENEES
ANDORRA
Pico de Aneto
11,168
Rhone
Garonne
Seine
Paris
Le Mans
Orléans
Tours
Nantes
Rennes
Le Havre
Rouen
Loire
Bordeaux
Bay of Biscay
San Sebastián
Bilbao
Pamplona
Ebro
Zaragoza
Vitoria
Valladolid
Santander
Gijón
La Coruña
Vigo
Braga
Porto
Coimbra
PORTUGAL
Lisbon
Setúbal
Badajoz
Guadiana
Córdoba
Sevilla
Cádiz
Strait of Gibraltar
Gibraltar (U.K.)
CAPE ST. VINCENT
IBERIAN
PENINSULA
SPAIN
Madrid
Toledo
Salamanca
León
Valencia
Alicante
Murcia
Cartagena
Almería
Granada
Málaga
Tagus
Duero

BALEARIC ISLANDS (Sp.)
MINORCA
MAJORCA
Palma
Barcelona

English Channel
Portsmouth
Plymouth
Dover
CHANNEL IS. (U.K.)
LAND'S END
Brest
Antwerp
Brussels
BELGIUM
Lille
Liège
LUXEMBOURG
Luxembourg

10°
40°
0°
10°
30°

MOROCCO
ALGERIA
TUNISIA

3
4
5
6

C
D
C
D

13

Russia, Ukraine, and Asia

A
GREENLAND
KALAALLIT NUNAAT
(DENMARK)

75°

FRANZ JOSEF LAND

NOVAYA
ZEMLYA

Kara Sea

Dikso

B
Arctic Circle

ICELAND

Norwegian Sea

• Murmansk

• Vorkuta

WEST

• Pechora

• Arkhangelsk

R SIBERIAN U

Ob

60°

North Sea

SWEDEN

FINLAND

Lake Onega

Lake Ladoga

St. Petersburg

Kirov •

Izhevsk •

• Perm

PLAIN

URAL MOUNTAINS

Irtysh

NORWAY

DENMARK

Baltic Sea

ESTONIA

LATVIA

LITHUANIA
(RUS.)

Moscow ⊗

• Nizhniy Novgorod

Volga

Kazan •

• Omsk

• Novosibi

UNITED KINGDOM

IRELAND

NETHERLANDS

BELGIUM

LUX.

GERMANY

POLAND

BELARUS

• Bryansk

Samara •

• Oral

Kama

KAZAKHSTAN

Pavlodar •

• Astana

• Semey

Novosibi

C

CZECH REP.

SLOVAKIA

• Lviv

• Kiev

UKRAINE

Volga

• Volgograd

• Novokazalinsk

• Qaraghandy

SWITZERLAND

AUSTRIA

HUNGARY

SLOVENIA

CROATIA

BOSNIA & HERZ.

SERBIA & MONT.

MOLDOVA

Donetsk •

• Rostov

Don

Sea of Azov

Aral Sea

Lake Balkhash

FRANCE

ROMANIA

• Odesa

Black Sea

CAUCASUS

• Almaty

SPAIN

ITALY

Adriatic Sea

ALBANIA

BULGARIA

F.Y.R. MAC.*

GEORGIA

Tbilisi ⊗

Caspian Sea

UZBEKISTAN

Bishkek ⊗

Sheng-Li Feng 24,406

D

Aegean Sea

GREECE

TURKEY

• Bursa

⊗ Ankara

ARMENIA

Yerevan ⊗

AZERBAIJAN

Baku •

Tashkent ⊗

KYRGYZSTAN

TAKLA MA

Mediterranean Sea

• Izmir

Mt. Ararat 16,804

AZER.

TURKMENISTAN

Communism Peak 24,590

TAKLA MA DESER

• Adana

Ashgabat ⊗

Dushanbe •

TAJIKISTAN

K2 28,250

TUNISIA

Nicosia ⊗

CYPRUS

Beirut ⊗

SYRIA

Teheran ⊗

Mt. Damavand 18,606

Mashhad •

Mazar-e Sharif •

KUNLUN MOUNTA

ALGERIA

LEBANON

ISRAEL

⊗ Damascus

Euphrates

Tigris

Baghdad •

• Esfahan

• Herat

Kabul •

Islamabad ⊗

PLATEAU OF TIBE

30°

Tel Aviv-Yafo •

Jerusalem ⊗

⊗ Amman

IRAQ

AFGHANISTAN

Lahore •

Srinagar •

WEST BANK*

JORDAN

• Al Basrah

Abadan •

IRAN

• Zahedan

Faisalabad •

HIM

GAZA STRIP*

KUWAIT

• Kuwait

PAKISTAN

Multan •

Delhi •

NEPAL

LIBYA

EGYPT

• Tabuk

Persian Gulf

• New Delhi

Kathmandu ⊗

Mt. Everes 29,03

SAUDI ARABIA

Manama ⊗

BAHRAIN

QATAR

⊗ Doha

• Dubayy

Abu Dhabi •

U.A.E.*

Muscat •

Karachi •

Kanpur •

Ganges

Patna •

Tropic of Cancer

Riyadh •

• Zahedan

OMAN

E

Jiddah •

Mecca •

ARABIAN PENINSULA

Arabian Sea

• Ahmedabad

INDIA

NIGER

CHAD

Red Sea

Mumbai (Bombay) •

• Vishakhapatnam

15°

ERITREA

YEMEN

Sanaa ⊗

• Al Mukalla

Hyderabad •

NIGERIA

SUDAN

• Aden

DJIBOUTI

SOCOTRA

• Bangalore

• Madras

ETHIOPIA

SOMALIA

Madurai •

F

CENTRAL AFRICAN REPUBLIC

SRI LANKA

CAMEROON

⊗ Colombo

MALDIVES

⊗ Male

EQUATORIAL GUINEA

UGANDA

REP. CONGO

0° *Equator*

GABON

KENYA

INDIAN OCEAN

DEM. REP. CONGO

RWANDA

BURUNDI

G

ANGOLA

TANZANIA

SEYCHELLES

DIEGO GARCIA *
(U.K.)

ANGOLA

ZAMBIA

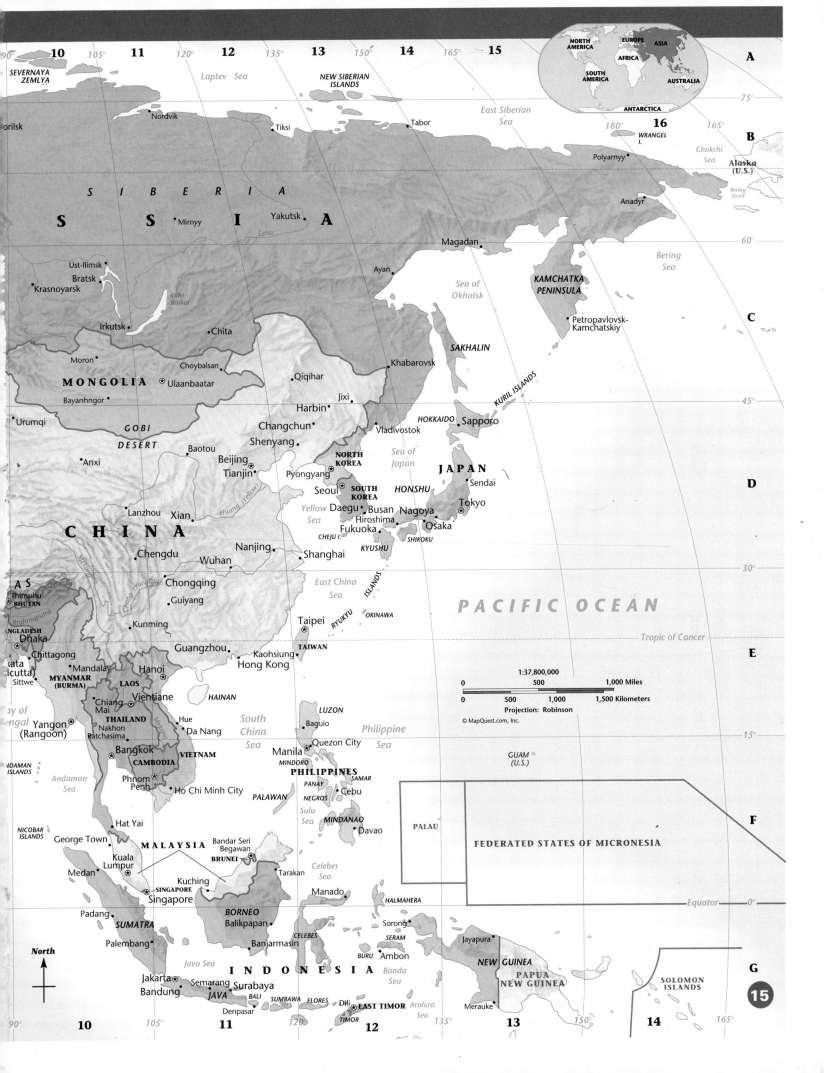

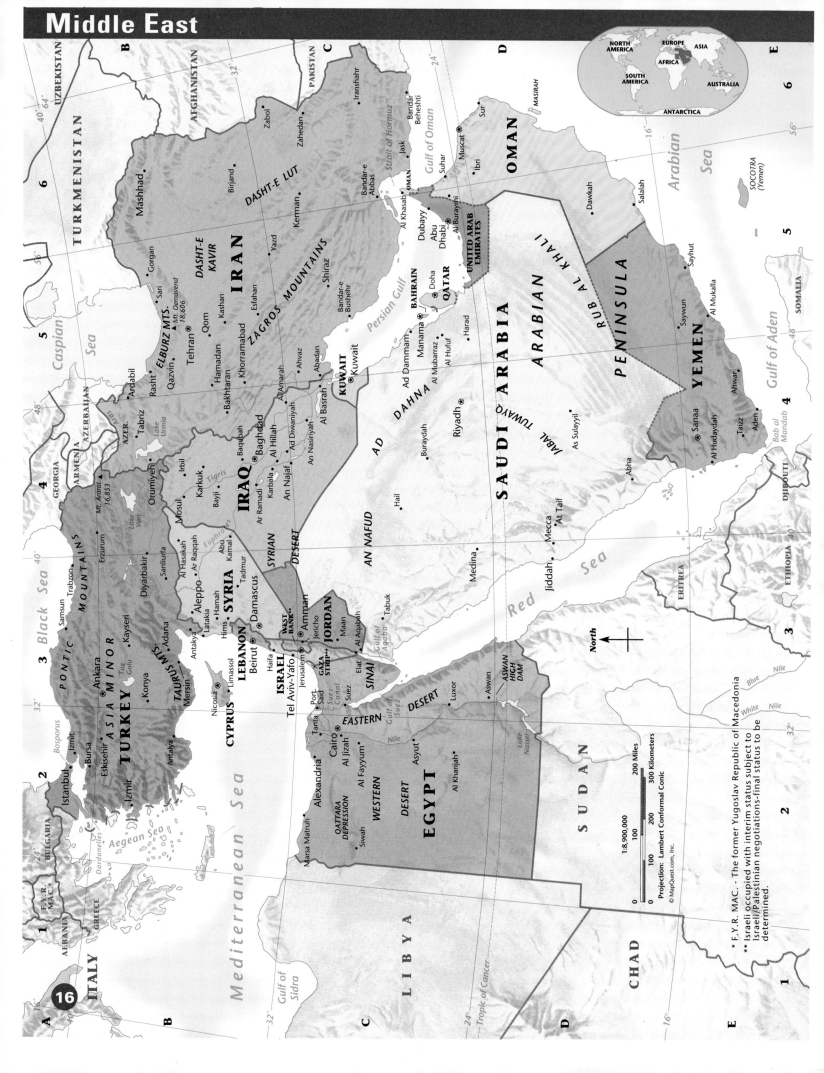

NORTH AMERICA · EUROPE · ASIA · AFRICA · SOUTH AMERICA · AUSTRALIA · ANTARCTICA

UZBEKISTAN
TURKMENISTAN
AFGHANISTAN
PAKISTAN

Mashhad
Zabol
Zahedan
Birjand
Iranshahr
Bandar Beheshti

DASHT-E LUT
IRAN
DASHT-E KAVIR

Gorgan
Sari
Mt. Demavend 18,606
Kerman
Yazd
Esfahan
Shiraz
Bandar-e Abbas
Strait of Hormuz

Tabriz
Ardabil
Rasht
Qazvin
Tehran
Qom
Hamadan
Kashan
Khorramabad
ELBURZ MTS.
ZAGROS MOUNTAINS

Bandar-e Bushehr
Persian Gulf

Orumiyeh
Lake Urmia
AZER.
ARMENIA
GEORGIA
Mt. Ararat 16,853

Ahvaz
Abadan
Al Amarah
KUWAIT
Kuwait

Jask
Sur
Muscat
Suhar
Ibri
OMAN
MASIRAH
Gulf of Oman
Arabian Sea
SOCOTRA (Yemen)

Al Khasab
OMAN
Dubayy
Abu Dhabi
Al Buraymi
UNITED ARAB EMIRATES
Doha
QATAR
BAHRAIN
Manama

RUB AL KHALI
ARABIAN PENINSULA
Dawkah
Salalah
Sayhut
Al Mukalla
Saywun

Caspian Sea
Black Sea
PONTIC MOUNTAINS
Samsun
Trabzon
Erzurum
Diyarbakir
Sanliurfa
Al Hasakah
Ar Raqqah
Mosul
Irbil
Karkuk
Bayji
Ar Ramadi
IRAQ
Baghdad
Baqubah
Karbala
An Najaf
Al Hillah
Ad Diwaniyah
An Nasiriyah
Al Basrah
Tigris
Euphrates

Ad Dammam
Ad Dahna
Al Mubarraz
Al Hufuf
Harad

AD DAHNA
SAUDI ARABIA
Riyadh
Buraydah
As Sulayyil
JABAL TUWAYQ

YEMEN
Sanaa
Al Hudaydah
Taizz
Aden
Ahwar
Bab al Mandab

SOMALIA
Gulf of Aden
DJIBOUTI
ERITREA
ETHIOPIA

BULGARIA
GREECE
ITALY
F.Y.R. MAC.*
ALBANIA

Istanbul
Izmit
Bursa
Eskisehir
Ankara
ASIA MINOR
TURKEY
Konya
Kayseri
Adana
Mersin
TAURUS MTS.
Antalya
Izmir
Tuz Golu
Antakya
Latakia
CYPRUS
Nicosia
Limassol

Aleppo
Hamah
Hims
SYRIA
Damascus
Tadmur
Ar Raqqah
Abu Kamal
SYRIAN DESERT

LEBANON
Beirut
ISRAEL
Haifa
Tel Aviv-Yafo
Jerusalem
WEST BANK**
Amman
JORDAN
Maan
GAZA STRIP**
Elat
Al Aqabah
Gulf of Aqaba
Jericho
Tabuk

SINAI
Port Said
Suez
Suez Canal
Gulf of Suez
EASTERN DESERT

EGYPT
Cairo
Al Jizah
Al Fayyum
Tanta
Alexandria
Marsa Matruh
Siwah
QATTARA DEPRESSION
WESTERN DESERT
Asyut
Al Kharijah
Luxor
Aswan
ASWAN HIGH DAM
Lake Nasser
Nile

Hail
Mecca
At Taif
Abha
Medina
Jiddah
AN NAFUD
Red Sea

SUDAN
LIBYA
CHAD
Gulf of Sidra
Mediterranean Sea
Aegean Sea
Bosporus
Dardanelles

North

Blue Nile
White Nile

1:8,900,000
0 100 200 Miles
0 100 200 300 Kilometers
Projection: Lambert Conformal Conic
© MapQuest.com, Inc.

* F.Y.R. MAC. - The former Yugoslav Republic of Macedonia
** Israeli occupied with interim status subject to Israeli/Palestinian negotiations-final status to be determined.

Tropic of Cancer

16

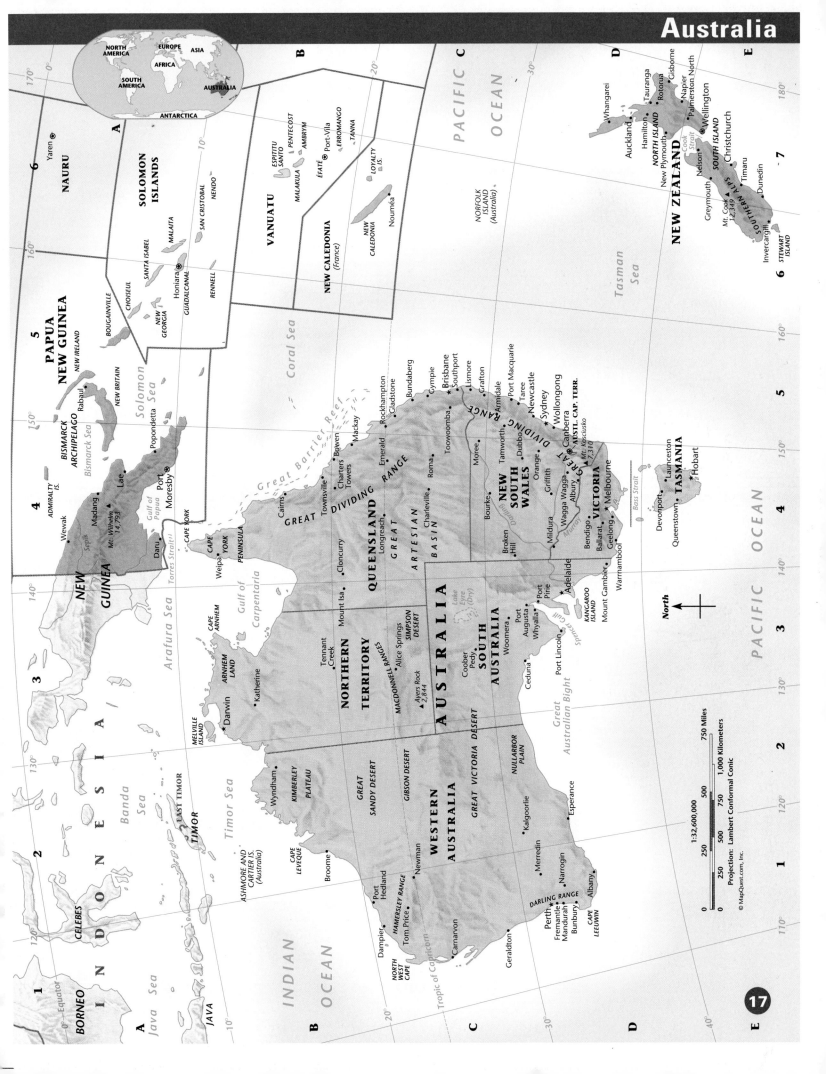

North Pole

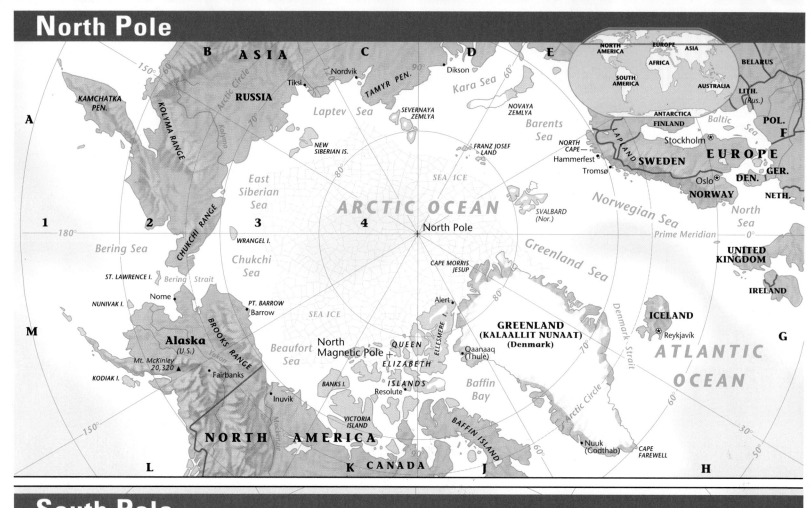

A — ASIA — B — C — D — E — F

KAMCHATKA PEN.

KOLYMA RANGE

RUSSIA

Tiksi · Nordvik

TAMYR PEN.

Dikson ·

Kara Sea

NORTH AMERICA EUROPE ASIA
AFRICA
SOUTH AMERICA AUSTRALIA
ANTARCTICA FINLAND BELARUS
LITH. (Rus.) POL.
SWEDEN EUROPE

Laptev Sea

SEVERNAYA ZEMLYA

NOVAYA ZEMLYA

Barents Sea

Stockholm

Arctic Circle

2

70

NEW SIBERIAN IS.

FRANZ JOSEF LAND

NORTH CAPE
Hammerfest ·

LAPLAND

GER.

East Siberian Sea

3

80

4

ARCTIC OCEAN

SEA/ICE

North Pole ·

SVALBARD (Nor.)

Tromsø ·

NORWAY

Oslo ⊛

DEN.

NETH.

1

180°

A — 180°

M

Bering Sea

WRANGEL I.

Chukchi Sea

CHUKCHI RANGE

ST. LAWRENCE I. Bering Strait

Nome ·

NUNIVAK I.

SEA ICE

Beaufort Sea

PT. BARROW
Barrow ·

North Magnetic Pole +

CAPE MORRIS JESUP

Alert ·

80

QUEEN ELIZABETH

ELLESMERE I.

Qaanaaq (Thule) ·

GREENLAND
(KALAALLIT NUNAAT)
(Denmark)

Greenland Sea

Denmark Strait

70

ICELAND

⊛ Reykjavík

Norwegian Sea

Prime Meridian 0°

North Sea

UNITED KINGDOM

IRELAND

ATLANTIC OCEAN

G

Alaska (U.S.)

BROOKS RANGE

Mt. McKinley 20,320 ▲

KODIAK I.

Fairbanks ·

Yokon

Inuvik ·

Mackenzie

BANKS I.

ISLANDS
Resolute ·

VICTORIA ISLAND

NORTH AMERICA

60

Baffin Bay

Baffin Island

Nuuk (Godthab) ·

Arctic Circle

60

CAPE FAREWELL

30°

50°

L — K CANADA — J — H

150°

South Pole

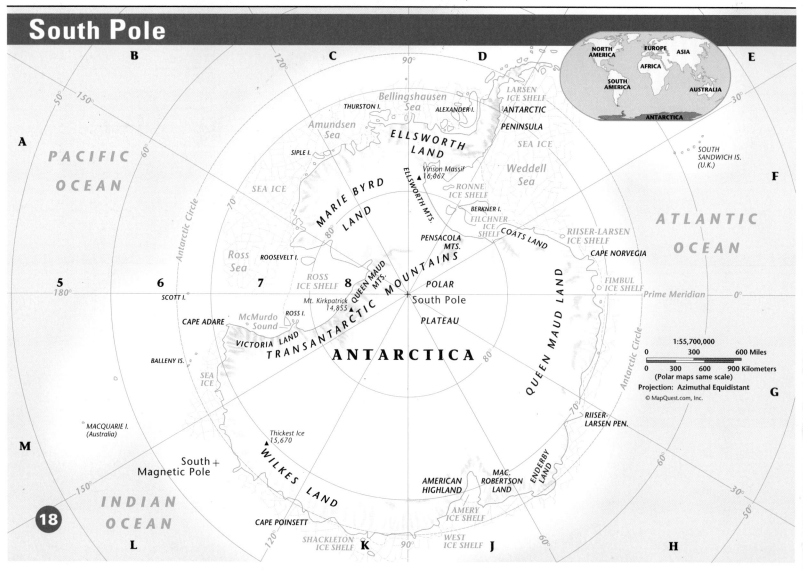

B — 120 — C — 90 — D — E

150

THURSTON I.

Bellingshausen Sea

ALEXANDER I.

LARSEN ICE SHELF

ANTARCTIC PENINSULA

NORTH AMERICA EUROPE ASIA
AFRICA
SOUTH AMERICA AUSTRALIA
ANTARCTICA

A

PACIFIC OCEAN

Amundsen Sea

SIPLE I.

ELLSWORTH LAND

Vinson Massif ▲ 16,067

SEA ICE

Weddell Sea

SOUTH SANDWICH IS. (U.K.)

F

60

MARIE BYRD LAND

ELLSWORTH MTS.

RONNE ICE SHELF

BERKNER I.

Antarctic Circle

70

SEA ICE

80

FILCHNER ICE SHELF

COATS LAND

RIISER-LARSEN ICE SHELF

ATLANTIC OCEAN

Ross Sea

ROOSEVELT I.

PENSACOLA MTS.

CAPE NORVEGIA

5

180°

6

SCOTT I.

7

ROSS ICE SHELF

8

QUEEN MAUD MTS.

Mt. Kirkpatrick 14,855 ▲

TRANSANTARCTIC MOUNTAINS

POLAR

South Pole +

PLATEAU

QUEEN MAUD LAND

FIMBUL ICE SHELF

Prime Meridian 0°

Antarctic Circle

CAPE ADARE

McMurdo Sound

ROSS I.

VICTORIA LAND

BALLENY IS.

SEA ICE

ANTARCTICA

1:55,700,000
0   300   600 Miles
0 300 600   900 Kilometers
(Polar maps same scale)
Projection: Azimuthal Equidistant
© MapQuest.com, Inc.

G

60

RIISER-LARSEN PEN.

MACQUARIE I. (Australia)

South + Magnetic Pole

Thickest Ice ▲ 15,670

WILKES LAND

AMERICAN HIGHLAND

MAC. ROBERTSON LAND

ENDERBY LAND

30°

M

150°

INDIAN OCEAN

18

CAPE POINSETT

SHACKLETON ICE SHELF

AMERY ICE SHELF

WEST ICE SHELF

50°

L — K — 120 — 90 — J — H

INDEX TO PLACES AND PHYSICAL FEATURES

Calais 5 7A
Calama 10 3E
Calgary 7 8C
Cali 10 2B
Callao 10 2D
Camagüey 8 2F
Cambridge Bay 6 9B
Camden 5 6B
Campbellton 7 13D
Campeche 8 3C
Campina Grande 10 6C
Campinas 10 5E
Campo Grande 10 4E
Canberra 17 4D
Cancún 8 4B
Canton 5 5A
Cap-Haïtien 8 2F
Cape Dorset 7 12B
Cape Girardeau 5 5B
Cape Town 11 5J
Caracas 10 3A
Carbondale 5 5B
Cardiff 13 3B
Carlsbad 4 3B
Carmacks 6 6B
Carnarvon 17 1C
Carson City 4 2B
Cartagena (Spain) 13 3D
Cartagena (Colombia) 10 2B
Cartwright 7 14C
Casa Grande 4 2B
Casablanca 11 3B
Casper 4 3A
Castries 8 4G
Catamarca 10 3E
Catania 13 5D
Caxias do Sul 10 4E
Cayenne 10 4B
Cebu 15 12F
Cedar City 4 2B
Cedar Rapids 5 4A
Ceduna 17 3D
Cerro de Pasco 10 2D
Ceuta 11 3B
Chadron 4 3A
Champaign 5 5B
Changchun 15 12D
Channel- Port aux Basques 7 14D
Charleston (S. Car., U.S.) 5 6B
Charleston (W. Va., U.S.) 5 5B
Charleville 17 4C
Charlotte 5 5B
Charlottesville 5 6B
Charlottetown 7 13D
Charters Towers 17 4C
Chatham 7 13D
Chattanooga 5 5B
Chemnitz 13 5B
Chengdu 15 10D
Chernivtsi 13 6C
Chesterfield Inlet 7 10B
Chetumal 8 4C
Cheyenne 4 3A
Chiang Mai 15 10E
Chibougamau 7 12D
Chicago 5 5A
Chiclayo 10 1C
Chicoutimi 7 12D
Chihuahua 8 2B
Chillán 10 2F
Chimbote 10 2C
Chimoio 11 7G
Chingola 11 6G
Chipata 11 7G
Chisasibi 7 12C
Chisinau 13 6C
Chita 15 11C
Chittagong 15 10E
Chongqing 15 11E
Choybalsan 15 11C
Christchurch 17 7E
Churchill 7 10C
Cienfuegos 8 1F
Cincinnati 5 5B
Ciudad Bolívar 10 3B
Ciudad de Valles 8 3B
Ciudad del Carmen 8 3C
Ciudad Guayana 10 3B
Ciudad Juárez 8 2A
Ciudad Mante 8 3B
Ciudad Obregón 8 2B
Ciudad Victoria 8 3B
Clarksville 5 5B
Clermont-Ferrand 13 4C
Cleveland 5 5A
Cloncurry 17 4C
Clovis 4 3B
Cluj- Napoca 13 6C
Coatzacoalcos 8 3C
Cobija 10 3D
Cochabamba 10 3D
Cody 4 3A
Coeur d'Alene 4 2A
Coimbra 13 3C
College 6 5B
Cologne 13 4B
Colombo 14 9F
Colón 8 5D
Colorado Springs 4 3B
Columbia (Mo., U.S.) 5 4B
Columbia (S. Car., U.S.) 5 5B
Columbus (Ga., U.S.) 5 5B
Columbus (Miss., U.S.) 5 5B
Columbus (Neb., U.S.) 4 4A
Columbus (Ohio, U.S.) 5 5B
Comitán 8 3C
Comodoro Rivadavia 10 3G
Conakry 11 2E
Concepción 10 2F
Concepción 10 4E
Concepción del Oro 8 2B
Concord 5 6A
Concordia 10 4F
Congo 11 5F
Constanta 13 6C
Constantine 11 4B
Coober Pedy 17 3C
Coos Bay 4 1A
Copenhagen 12 5B
Copiapó 10 2E
Córdoba (Spain) 13 3D
Córdoba (Argentina) 10 3F
Cordova 6 5B
Corinth 13 6D
Cork 12 3B
Corner Brook 7 14D
Coro 10 3A
Coronel Oviedo 10 4E
Corpus Christi 4 4C
Corrientes 10 4E
Corumbá 10 4D
Corvallis 4 1A
Côte d'Ivoire 11 3E
Council Bluffs 5 4A
Coventry 12 3B
Craig 4 3A
Craiova 13 6C
Cruzeiro do Sul 10 2C
Cúcuta 10 2B
Cuenca 10 2C
Cuernavaca 8 3C
Cuiabá 10 4D
Culiacán 8 2B
Cumaná 10 3A
Cumberland 5 6B
Curitiba 10 5E
Cuzco 10 2D
Da Nang 15 11E
Daegu 15 12D
Dakar 11 2D
Dallas 5 4B
Damascus 16 3B
Dampier 17 1C
Danville 5 6B
Dar es Salaam 11 7F
Dartmouth 7 13D
Daru 17 4A
Darwin 17 3B
Daugavpils 12 6B
Dauphin 7 10C
Davao 15 12F
Davenport 5 4A
David 8 4D
Dawkah 16 5D
Dawson 6 6B
Dawson Creek 6 5C
Dayton 5 5B
Daytona Beach 5 5C
Debrecen 13 6C
Decatur 5 5B
Del Rio 4 3C
Delhi 14 9E
Delicias 8 2B
Denpasar 15 11G
Denver 4 3B
Des Moines 5 4A
Dese 11 7D
Detroit 5 5A
Devonport 17 4E
Dhaka 15 10E
Dickinson 4 3A
Dijon 13 4C
Dikson 14 9B
Diline 6 7B
Dillingham 6 4C
Dire Dawa 11 8E
Diyarbakir 16 3B
Djibouti 11 8D
Dodge City 4 3B
Dodoma 11 7F
Doha 16 5C
Donetsk 14 6C
Dothan 5 5B
Douala 11 4E
Dourados 10 4E
Dover 13 4B
Dover 5 6B
Drammen 12 5B
Dresden 13 5B
Dubayy 16 5C
Dubbo 17 4D
Dublin 12 3B
Dubrovnik 13 5C
Dubuque 5 4A
Duluth 5 4A
Dundee 12 3B
Dunedin 17 7E
Durango (Mexico) 8 2B
Durango (Colo., U.S.) 4 3B
Durant 4 4B
Durban 11 7H
Durham 5 6B
Durrës 13 5C
Dushanbe 14 8D
East London 11 6J
Eau Claire 5 4A
Edinburgh 12 3B
Edmonton 6 8C
Edmundston 7 13D
Edzo 6 8B
El Aaiún 11 2C
El Asnam 11 4B
El Dorado 5 4B
El Paso 4 3B
El Tigre 10 3B
Elat 16 3C
Eldoret 11 7E
Elko 4 2A
Ely 4 2B
Emerald 17 4C
Emporia 5 4B
Encarnación 10 4E
Enid 4 4B
Ensenada 8 1A
Enugu 11 4E
Erfurt 13 5B
Erie 5 5A
Erzurum 16 4B
Esbjerg 12 4B
Escanaba 5 5A
Escuintla 8 3C
Esfahan 16 5B
Eskisehir 16 2B
Esmeraldas 10 2B
Esperance 17 2D
Esquel 10 2G
Essen 13 4B
Eugene 4 1A
Eureka 4 1A
Evansville 5 5B
Everett 4 1A
Fairbanks 6 5B
Faisalabad 14 8D
Fargo 4 4A
Farmington 4 3B
Faya-Largeau 11 5D
Fayetteville (Ark., U.S.) 5 4B
Fayetteville (N. Car., U.S.) 5 6B
Feira de Santana 10 6D
Fès 11 3B
Fianarantsoa 11 8H
Flagstaff 4 2B
Flin Flon 6 9C
Flint 5 5A
Florence 13 5C
Florence (Ala., U.S.) 5 5B
Florence (S. Car., U.S.) 5 6B
Florencia 10 2B
Floriano 10 5C
Florianópolis 10 5E
Foggia 13 5C
Formosa 10 4E
Fort Albany 7 11C
Fort Collins 4 3A
Fort Dodge 5 4A
Fort Francis 7 10D
Fort Lauderdale 5 5C
Fort Liard 6 7B
Fort McMurray 6 8C
Fort McPherson 6 6B
Fort Myers 5 5C
Fort Nelson 6 7C
Fort Pierce 5 5C
Fort Severn 7 11C
Fort Simpson 6 7B
Fort Smith (N.W.T., Can.) 6 8B
Fort Smith (Ark., U.S.) 5 4B
Fort St. John 6 7C
Fort Stockton 4 3B
Fort Vermilion 6 8C
Fort Wayne 5 5A
Fort Worth 4 4B
Fort Yukon 6 5B
Fort-de-France 8 4G
Fortaleza 10 6C
Franceville 11 5F
Francistown 11 6H
Frankfort 5 5B
Frankfurt 13 4B
Fredericton 7 13D
Freeport 8 2E
Freetown 11 2E
Fremantle 17 1D
Fresnillo 8 2B
Fresno 4 2B
Fukuoka 15 12D
Funchal 11 2B
Gaborone 11 6H
Gadsden 5 5B
Gainesville 5 5C
Galati 13 6C
Gallup 4 3B
Galveston 5 4C
Galway 12 3B
Gander 7 14D
Gao 11 4D
Garoua 11 5E
Gary 5 5A
Gdansk 12 5B
Geelong 17 4D
Geneva 13 4C
Genoa 13 4C
George Town (Malaysia) 15 10F
George Town (Cayman Is.) 8 1F
Georgetown 10 4B
Geraldton 17 1C
Ghadamis 11 4B
Ghardaïa 11 4B
Gibraltar (U.K.) 13 3D
Gijón 13 3C
Gillam 7 10C
Gisborne 17 7D
Gjoa Haven 7 10B
Gladstone 17 5C
Glasgow (Scot., U.K.) 12 3B
Glasgow (Mont., U.S.) 4 3A
Goiânia 10 5D
Goma 11 6F
Gonaïves 8 2F
Gonder 11 7D
Gorgan 16 5B
Göteborg 12 5B
Governador Valadares 10 5D
Grafton 17 5C
Granada (Spain) 13 3D
Granada (Nicaragua) 8 4C
Grand Falls-Windsor 7 14D
Grand Forks 4 4A
Grand Island 4 4A
Grand Junction 4 3B
Grand Prairie 6 8C
Grand Rapids (Man., Can.) 7 10C
Grand Rapids (Mich., U.S.) 5 5A
Graz 13 5C
Great Falls 4 2A
Greeley 4 3A
Green Bay 5 5A
Greensboro 5 6B
Greenville (Miss., U.S.) 5 4B
Greenville (S. Car., U.S.) 5 5B
Grenoble 13 4C
Greymouth 17 7E
Griffith 17 4D
Grise Fiord 7 11A
Groningen 12 4B
Guadalajara 8 2B
Guajará-Mirim 10 3D
Guangzhou 15 11E
Guantánamo 8 2F
Guatemala 8 3C
Guayaquil 10 1C
Guaymas 8 1B
Guiyang 15 11E
Gurupi 10 5D
Gweru 11 6G
Gympie 17 5C
Gyor 13 5C
Hagerstown 5 6B
Haifa 16 3B
Hail 16 4C
Haines 6 6C
Halifax 7 13D
Halmstad 12 5B
Hamadan 16 5B
Hamah 16 3B
Hamburg 12 5B
Hamilton (New Zealand) 17 7D
Hamilton (Ont., Can.) 7 12D
Hammerfest 12 6A
Hannibal 5 4B
Hannover 12 4B
Hanoi 15 11E
Happy Valley- Goose Bay 7 13C
Harad 16 5C
Harare 11 7G
Harbin 15 12D
Harer 11 8E
Hargeysa 11 8E
Harrisburg 5 6B
Hartford 5 6A
Hat Yai 15 10F
Hattiesburg 5 5B
Haugesund 12 4B
Havana 8 1F
Havre 4 3A
Havre- St. Pierre 7 13C
Hawthorne 4 2B
Hay River 6 8B
Hays 4 4B
Hebron 7 13C
Helena 4 2A
Helsingborg 12 5B
Helsinki 12 6A
Henderson 4 2B
Herat 14 8D
Hermosillo 8 1B
Hibbing 5 4A
Hidalgo del Parral 8 2B
Hilo 4 2C
Hims 16 3B
Hiroshima 15 12D
Ho Chi Minh City 15 11F
Hobart 17 4E
Holguín 8 2F
Holy Cross 6 4B
Homer 6 4C
Homyel 12 7B
Hong Kong 15 11E
Honiara 17 5A
Honolulu 4 2C
Hopedale 7 13C
Hot Springs 5 4B
Houghton 5 5A
Houlton 5 7A
Houston 5 4C
Hrodna 12 6B
Huambo 11 5G
Huancayo 10 2D
Huánuco 10 2C
Hue 15 11E
Hull 7 12D
Huntington 5 5B
Huntsville 5 5B
Hutchison 4 4B
Hyderabad 14 9E
I-n-Amenas 11 4C
I-n-Salah 11 4C
Iasi 13 6C
Ibadan 11 4E
Ibagué 10 2B
Ibri 16 6D
Ica 10 2D
Idaho Falls 4 2A
Ilebo 11 6F
Ilhéus 10 6D
Ilorin 11 4E
Imperatriz 10 5C
Indianapolis 5 5B
Inhambane 11 7H
Innsbruck 13 5C
International Falls 5 4A
Inuvik 6 6B
Invercargill 17 6E
Inverness 12 3B
Ioánnina 13 6D
Iqaluit 7 13B
Iquique 10 2E
Iquitos 10 2C
Iráklion 13 6D
Iranshahr 16 6C
Irapuato 8 2B
Irbil 16 4B
Iringa 11 7F
Irkutsk 15 10C
Isafjördhur 12 1A
Isiro 11 6E
Islamabad 14 8D
Istanbul 16 2A
Itabuna 10 6D
Ithaca 5 6A
Ivalo 12 6A
Izhevsk 14 7C
Izmir 14 5D
Izmir 16 2B
Izmit 16 2A
Jackson (Miss., U.S.) 5 4B
Jackson (Tenn., U.S.) 5 5B
Jackson (Wyo., U.S.) 4 2A
Jacksonville 5 5B
Jakarta 15 11G
Jamestown (N.Y., U.S.) 5 6A
Jamestown (N. Dak., U.S.) 4 4A
Jask 16 6C
Jasper 6 8C
Jataí 10 4D
Jayapura 15 13G
Jefferson City 5 4B
Jericho 16 3C
Jerusalem 16 3C
Jiddah 16 3D
Jima 11 7E
Jinja 11 7E
Jixi 15 12C
João Pessoa 10 6C
Johannesburg 11 6H
Johnson City 5 5B
Joinvile 10 5E
Joliet 5 5A
Jonesboro 5 4B
Jönköping 12 5B
Joplin 5 4B
Juàzeiro do Norte 10 6C
Juba 11 7E
Juiz de Fora 10 5E
Juliaca 10 2D
Jundiaí 10 5E
Juneau 6 6C
Junín 10 3F
Jyvaskyla 12 6A
Kabinda 11 6F
Kabul 14 8D
Kabwe 11 6G
Kahului 4 2C
Kailua-Kona 4 2C
Kalámai 13 6D
Kalamazoo 5 5A
Kalemie 11 6F
Kalgoorlie 17 2D
Kaliningrad 12 6B
Kalispell 4 2A
Kamina 11 6F
Kamloops 6 7C
Kampala 11 7E
Kananga 11 6F
Kankan 11 3D
Kano 11 4D
Kanpur 14 9E
Kansas City (Kan., U.S.) 5 4B
Kansas City (Mo., U.S.) 5 4B
Kaohsiung 15 12E
Kaolack 11 2D
Karachi 14 8E
Karbala 16 4B
Karkuk 16 4B
Karlstad 12 5B
Kashan 16 5B
Kassala 11 7D
Kassel 13 4B
Katherine 17 3B
Kathmandu 14 9E
Katowice 13 5B
Katsina 11 4D
Kaunas 12 6B
Kavalá 13 6C
Kayes 11 2D
Kayseri 16 3B
Kazan 14 7C
Kearney 4 4A
Kecskemet 13 5C
Keetmanshoop 11 5H
Keflavík 12 1A
Kelafo 11 8E
Kelowna 6 8D
Kenai 6 4B
Kennewick 4 2A
Kenora 7 10D
Kerman 16 6C
Ketchikan 6 6C
Key West 5 5C
Khabarovsk 15 13C
Khaniá 13 6D
Khartoum 11 7D
Khorramabad 16 5B
Kiel 12 5B
Kielce 13 6B
Kiev 14 6C
Kigali 11 7F
Kikwit 11 5F
Killeen 4 4B
Kimberley 11 6H
Kindu 11 6F
Kingman 4 2B
Kingston (Ont., Can.) 7 12D
Kingston (Jamaica) 8 2F
Kingston upon Hull 12 3B
Kingstown 8 4G

Kinshasa	11	5F
Kirov	14	7C
Kiruna	12	6A
Kisangani	11	6E
Kismaayo	11	8F
Kisumu	11	7F
Kitchener	7	11D
Kitimat	6	7C
Kitwe	11	6G
Klagenfurt	13	5C
Klaipeda	12	6B
Klamath Falls	4	1A
Klerksdorp	11	6H
Knoxville	5	5B
Kodiak	6	4C
Kolkata (Calcutta)	15	9E
Kolwezi	11	6G
Konya	16	3B
Korhogo	11	3E
Kosice	13	6C
Kotka	12	6A
Kotzebue	6	3B
Kourou	10	4B
Krakow	13	5B
Krasnoyarsk	15	10C
Kristiansand	12	4B
Kuala Lumpur	15	10F
Kuching	15	11F
Kugluktuk	6	8B
Kumasi	11	3E
Kumo	11	5D
Kunming	15	10E
Kuopio	12	6A
Kuqa	14	9D
Kuraymah	11	7D
Kusti	11	7D
Kuujjuaq	7	13C
Kuujjuarapik	7	12C
Kuwait	16	4C
La Ceiba	8	4C
La Coruña	13	3C
La Crosse	5	4A
La Junta	4	3B
La Loche	6	9C
La Paz (Mexico)	8	1B
La Paz (Bolivia)	10	3D
La Plata	10	4F
La Rioja	10	3E
La Ronge	6	9C
La Serena	10	2E
Labé	11	2D
Labrador City	7	13C
Lae	17	4A
Lafayette (Ind., U.S.)	5	5A
Lafayette (La., U.S.)	5	4B
Lagos	11	4E
Lahore	14	8D
Lahti	12	6A
Lake Charles	5	4B
Lambaréné	11	5F
Lander	4	3A
Lansing	5	5A
Lanzhou	15	10D
Laramie	4	3A
Laredo	4	4C
Lárisa	13	6D
Las Cruces	4	3B
Las Palmas	11	2C
Las Vegas (Nev., U.S.)	4	2B
Las Vegas (N. Mex., U.S.)	4	3B
Latakia	16	3B
Launceston	17	4E
Lawrence	5	4B
Lawton	4	4B
Lázaro Cárdenas	8	2C
Le Havre	13	4C
Le Mans	13	4C
Leeds	12	3B
Leipzig	13	5B
León (Spain)	13	3C
León (Mexico)	8	2B
León (Nicaragua)	8	4C
Lethbridge	6	8D
Lewiston (Id., U.S.)	4	2A
Lewiston (Maine, U.S.)	5	6A
Lexington	5	5B
Liberec	13	5B
Libreville	11	4E
Liège	13	4B
Liepaja	12	6B
Lihue	4	2C
Likasi	11	6G
Lille	13	4B
Lilongwe	11	7G
Lima	10	2D
Limassol	16	3B
Limerick	12	3B
Limoges	13	4C
Lincoln	5	4A
Linköping	12	5B
Linz	13	5C
Lisbon	13	3D
Lismore	17	5C
Little Rock	5	4B
Liverpool	12	3B
Livingstone	11	6G
Ljubljana	13	5C
Lobito	11	5G
Lodz	13	5B
Logan	4	2A
Loja	10	2C
Lomé	11	4E
London (Ont., Can.)	7	11D
London (Eng., U.K.)	13	4B
Londonderry	12	3B
Londrina	10	4E
Long Beach	4	2B
Longreach	17	4C
Longview	5	4B
Loreto	8	1B
Los Angeles	4	2B
Los Mochis	8	2B
Louisville	5	5B
Luanda	11	5F
Luanshya	11	6G
Lubango	11	5G
Lubbock	4	3B
Lübeck	12	5B
Lublin	13	6B
Lubumbashi	11	6G
Lüderitz	11	5H
Luena	11	5G
Lufkin	5	4B
Luleå	12	6A
Lusaka	11	6G
Luxembourg	13	4C
Luxor	16	3C
Lviv	14	5C
Lyon	13	4C
Maan	16	3C
Macapá	10	4B
Maceió	10	6C
Machakos	11	7F
Machala	10	1C
Mackay	17	4C
Macon	5	5B
Madang	17	4A
Madgeburg	13	5B
Madison	5	5A
Madras	14	9F
Madrid	13	3C
Madurai	14	9F
Magadan	15	14C
Mahajanga	11	8G
Mahilyow	12	7B
Maiduguri	11	5D
Makurdi	11	4E
Malabo	11	4E
Malaga	13	3D
Malakal	11	7E
Malanje	11	5F
Male	14	8F
Malmö	12	5B
Manado	15	12F
Managua	8	4C
Manama	16	5C
Manaus	10	4C
Manchester (Eng., U.K.)	12	3B
Manchester (N. Hamp., U.S.)	5	6A
Mandalay	15	10E
Mandurah	17	1D
Manhattan	4	4B
Manila	15	12F
Manizales	10	2B
Mankato	5	4A
Mannheim	13	4C
Mansfield	5	5A
Manzanillo	8	2F
Maputo	11	7H
Mar del Plata	10	4F
Maracaibo	10	2A
Maracay	10	3B
Maradi	11	4D
Marietta	5	5B
Marka	11	8E
Maroua	11	5D
Marquette	5	5A
Marrakech	11	3B
Marsa Matruh	16	2C
Marsabit	11	7E
Marseille	13	4C
Maseru	11	6H
Mashhad	16	6B
Mason City	5	4A
Massawa	11	7D
Matadi	11	5F
Matamoros	8	3B
Matanzas	8	1F
Maturín	10	3B
Mayagüez	8	3F
Mazar-e Sharif	14	8D
Mazatlán	8	2B
Mbabane	11	7H
Mbala	11	7F
Mbandaka	11	5E
Mbanza- Ngungu	11	5F
Mbeya	11	7F
Mbuji-Mayi	11	6F
McAlester	5	4B
McAllen	4	4C
Mecca	16	3D
Medan	15	10F
Medellín	10	2B
Medford	4	1A
Medicine Hat	6	8C
Medina	16	3C
Mekele	11	7D
Melbourne (Vict., Austl.)	17	4D
Melbourne (Flor., U.S.)	5	5C
Melilla	11	3B
Melo	10	4F
Memphis	5	5B
Mendoza	10	3F
Menongue	11	5G
Merauke	15	13G
Mérida (Mexico)	8	4B
Mérida (Venezuela)	10	2B
Meridian (Miss., U.S.)	5	5B
Merredin	17	1D
Mersin	16	3B
Meru	11	7E
Messina (South Africa)	11	7H
Messina (Italy)	13	5D
Mexicali	8	1A
México City	8	3C
Miami	5	5C
Middelburg	11	6J
Midland	4	3B
Milan	13	4C
Mildura	17	4D
Miles City	4	3A
Milwaukee	5	5A
Minas	10	4F
Minna	11	4E
Minneapolis	5	4A
Minot	4	3A
Minsk	12	6B
Mirnyy	15	11B
Miskolc	13	5C
Misratah	11	5B
Missoula	4	2A
Mittimatalik	7	12A
Moab	4	3B
Mobile	5	5B
Mobridge	4	3A
Mogadishu	11	8E
Molde	12	4A
Mombasa	11	7F
Monclova	8	2B
Moncton	7	13D
Monroe	5	4B
Monrovia	11	2E
Montego Bay	8	2F
Monterey	4	1B
Montería	10	2B
Monterrey	8	2B
Montes Claros	10	5D
Montevideo	10	4F
Montgomery	5	5B
Montpelier	5	6A
Montpellier	13	4C
Montréal	7	12D
Montrose	4	3B
Moose Jaw	6	9C
Moosonee	7	11C
Mopti	11	3D
Moree	17	4C
Morelia	8	2C
Morgan City	5	4C
Morgantown	5	5B
Morogoro	11	7F
Moron	15	10C
Moroni	11	8G
Moscow	14	6C
Mosul	16	4B
Moulmein	15	10E
Moundou	11	5E
Mount Gambier	17	4D
Mount Isa	17	3C
Mount Pleasant	5	5A
Mtwara	11	8G
Multan	14	8D
Mumbai (Bombay)	14	8E
Muncie	5	5B
Munich	13	5C
Murcia	13	3D
Murmansk	14	6B
Muscat	16	6D
Muskegon	5	5A
Muskogee	5	4B
Mutare	11	7G
Mwanza	11	7F
Mwene Ditu	11	6F
Myrtle Beach	5	6B
N'Djamena	11	5D
Nacala	11	8G
Nagoya	15	13D
Nain	7	13C
Nairobi	11	7F
Nakhon Ratchasima	15	10E
Nakuru	11	7F
Namibe	11	5G
Nampula	11	7G
Namsos	12	5A
Nanaimo	6	7D
Nancy	13	4C
Nanjing	15	11D
Nantes	13	3C
Napier	17	7D
Naples (Italy)	13	5C
Naples (Flor., U.S.)	5	5C
Narrogin	17	1D
Narvik	12	5A
Nashville	5	5B
Nassau	8	2E
Natal	10	6C
Natchez	5	4B
Navojoa	8	2B
Nazret	11	7E
Ndola	11	6G
Necochea	10	4F
Neiva	10	2B
Nelson	17	7E
Neuquén	10	3F
New Amsterdam	10	4B
New Bedford	5	6A
New Bern	5	6B
New Delhi	14	9E
New Glasgow	7	13D
New Haven	5	6A
New Orleans	5	4C
New Plymouth	17	7D
New York	5	6A
Newark	5	6A
Newcastle (N.S.W., Austl.)	17	5D
Newcastle (Eng., U.K.)	12	3B
Newman	17	1C
Newport News	5	6B
Niamey	11	4D
Nice	13	4C
Nicosia	16	3B
Nipigon	7	11D
Nis	13	6C
Niterói	10	5E
Nizhniy Novgorod	14	6C
Nogales	8	1A
Nogales	4	2B
Nome	6	3B
Nordvik	15	11B
Norfolk	5	6B
Norilsk	15	9B
Norrköping	12	5B
North Bay	7	12D
North Platte	4	3A
Norwich	12	4B
Nottingham	12	3B
Nouadhibou	11	2C
Nouakchott	11	2D
Nouméa	17	6C
Novgorod	12	7B
Novi Sad	13	5C
Novokazalinsk	14	8C
Novosibirsk	14	9C
Nueva Casas Grandes	8	2A
Nueva Gerona	8	1F
Nuevo Laredo	8	3B
Nürnberg	13	5C
Nyala	11	6D
Oakland	4	1B
Oaxaca	8	3C
Ocala	5	5C
Odense	12	5B
Odesa	14	6C
Odessa	4	3B
Ogbomosho	11	4E
Ogden	4	2A
Oklahoma City	4	4B
Olympia	4	1A
Omaha	5	4A
Omdurman	11	7D
Omsk	14	8C
Onitsha	11	4E
Oradea	13	6C
Oral	14	7C
Oran	11	3B
Orange	17	4D
Oranjestad	8	3G
Örebro	12	5B
Orlando	5	5C
Orléans	13	4C
Orumiyeh	16	4B
Oruro	10	3D
Osaka	15	13D
Oshawa	7	12D
Oshogbo	11	4E
Oslo	12	5A
Osorno	10	2G
Östersund	12	5A
Ostrava	13	5C
Ottawa	7	12D
Ottumwa	5	4A
Ouagadougou	11	3D
Oujda	11	3B
Oulo	12	6A
Owensboro	5	5B
Padang	15	10G
Paducah	5	5B
Palapye	11	6H
Palembang	15	10G
Palermo	13	5D
Palma	13	4D
Palmerston North	17	7E
Palmira	10	2B
Pamplona	13	3C
Panamá	8	5D
Panama City	5	5B
Pangnirtung	7	13B
Paramaribo	10	4B
Paraná	10	3F
Paris (France)	13	4C
Paris (Texas, U.S.)	5	4B
Parkersburg	5	5B
Parma	13	5C
Parnaíba	10	5C
Passo Fundo	10	4E
Pasto	10	2B
Paterson	5	6A
Patna	14	9E
Pátrai	13	6D
Pavlodar	14	9C
Paysandú	10	4F
Peace River	6	8C
Pechora	14	7B
Pecs	13	5C
Pelotas	10	4F
Pendleton	4	2A
Pensacola	5	5B
Peoria	5	5A
Pereira	10	2B
Perm	14	7C
Perth	17	1D
Peterborough	7	12D
Petersburg	5	6B
Petrolina	10	5C
Petropavlovsk- Kamchatskiy	15	14C
Petrozavodsk	12	7A
Philadelphia	5	6B
Phnom Penh	15	11F
Phoenix	4	2B
Pierre	4	3A
Pietermaritzburg	11	7H
Pinar del Río	8	1F
Pine Bluff	5	4B
Pisa	13	5C
Pittsburgh	5	5A
Piura	10	1C
Plainview	4	3B
Pleven	13	6C
Ploiesti	13	6C
Plovdiv	13	6C
Plymouth	13	3B
Plzen	13	5C
Pocatello	4	2A
Podgorica	13	5C
Point Hope	6	3B
Pointe-à-Pitre	8	4F
Pointe-Noire	11	5F
Polyarnyy	15	15B
Ponce	8	3F
Pond Inlet	7	12A
Ponta Grossa	10	4E
Popayán	10	2B
Poplar Bluff	5	4B
Popondetta	17	4A
Pori	12	6A
Port Augusta	17	3D
Port Elizabeth	11	6J
Port Harcourt	11	4E
Port Hedland	17	1C
Port Lincoln	17	3D
Port Macquarie	17	5D
Port Moresby	17	4A
Port Pirie	17	3D
Port Said	11	7B
Port Said	16	3C
Port Sudan	11	7D
Port- Gentil	11	4F
Port-au-Prince	8	2F
Port-of-Spain	8	4G
Port-Vila	17	6B
Portland (Maine, U.S.)	5	6A
Portland (Ore., U.S.)	4	1A
Porto	13	3C
Pôrto Alegre	10	4F
Pôrto Velho	10	3C
Porto-Novo	11	4E
Portoviejo	10	1C
Portsmouth (Eng., U.K.)	13	3B
Portsmouth (N. Hamp., U.S.)	5	6A
Portsmouth (Va., U.S.)	5	6B
Posadas	10	4E
Potosí	10	3E
Povungnituk	7	12B
Poza Rica	8	3B
Poznan	12	5B
Prague	13	5B
Prescott	4	2B
Presidente Prudente	10	4E
Presque Isle	5	7A
Pretoria	11	6H
Prince Albert	6	9C
Prince George	6	7C
Prince Rupert	6	6C
Providence	5	6A
Provo	4	2A
Prudhoe Bay	6	5A
Pskov	12	6B
Pucallpa	10	2C
Puebla	8	3C
Pueblo	4	3B
Puerto Ayacucho	10	3B
Puerto Escondido	8	3C
Puerto Limón	8	4D
Puerto Maldonado	10	3D
Puerto Montt	10	2G
Puerto Peñasco	8	1A
Puno	10	2D
Punta Alta	10	3F
Punta Arenas	10	2H
Puntarenas	8	4C
Pyongyang	15	12D
Qaraghandy	14	8C
Qazvin	16	5B
Qiqihar	15	12C
Qom	16	5B
Québec	7	12D
Queenstown	17	4E
Quelimane	11	7G
Querétaro	8	2B
Quezon City	15	12F
Quincy	5	4B
Quito	10	2B
Rabat	11	3B
Rabaul	17	5A
Racine	5	5A
Radom	13	6B
Raleigh	5	6B
Rancagua	10	2F
Rankin Inlet	7	10B
Rapid City	4	3A
Rasht	16	5B
Rawson	10	3G
Reading	5	6A
Recife	10	6C
Reconquista	10	4E
Red Deer	6	8C
Redding	4	1A
Regensburg	13	5C
Reggio di Calabria	13	5D
Regina	6	9C
Rennes	13	3C
Reno	4	2B
Repulse Bay	7	11B
Resistencia	10	4E
Resolute	7	10A
Reykjavík	12	1A
Reynosa	8	3B
Ribeirão Prêto	10	5E
Riberalta	10	3D
Richfield	4	2B
Richmond	5	6B
Riga	12	6B
Rijeka	13	5C
Rimouski	7	13D
Rio Branco	10	3C
Río Cuarto	10	3F
Rio de Janeiro	10	5E
Río Gallegos	10	3H
Rivera	10	4F
Riverside	4	2B
Riyadh	14	7E
Riyadh	16	4C
Roanoke	5	6B
Rochester (Minn., U.S.)	5	4A
Rochester (N.Y., U.S.)	5	6A
Rock Island	5	4A

PHYSICAL FEATURES

Geography Terms

1. **basin** bowl-shaped area of land surrounded by higher land

2. **bay** an inlet of the sea or some other body of water, usually smaller than a gulf

3. **bluff** high, steep face of rock or earth

4. **canyon** deep, narrow valley with steep sides

5. **cape** point of land that extends into water

6. **cataract** large waterfall

7. **channel** deepest part of a body of water

8. **cliff** high, steep face of rock or earth

9. **coast** land along a sea or ocean

10. **coastal plain** area of flat land along a sea or ocean

11. **delta** triangle-shaped area of land at the mouth of a river

12. **desert** dry land with few plants

13. **dune** hill of sand piled up by the wind

14. **fall line** area along which rivers form waterfalls or rapids as the rivers drop to lower land

15. **floodplain** flat land that is near the edges of a river and is formed by silt deposited by floods

16. **foothills** hilly area at the base of a mountain

17. **glacier** large ice mass that moves slowly down a mountain or across land

18. **gulf** part of a sea or ocean extending into the land, usually larger than a bay

19. **hill** land that rises above the land around it

20. **inlet** any area of water extending into the land from a larger body of water

21. **island** land that has water on all sides

22. **isthmus** narrow strip of land connecting two larger areas of land

23. **lagoon** body of shallow water

24. **lake** body of water with land on all sides

25. **marsh** lowland with moist soil and tall grasses